It's an Inside Job

The Journal

Seven Dimensions of Wellness LLC

You matter.

This journal is dedicated to you, the writer.

Your thoughts, your emotions, your experiences—they all hold significance.

Through the art of journaling, may you uncover the depth of your inner world and embrace the power of your voice.

I am curious,
aware, and always
learning—I have the
power to create.

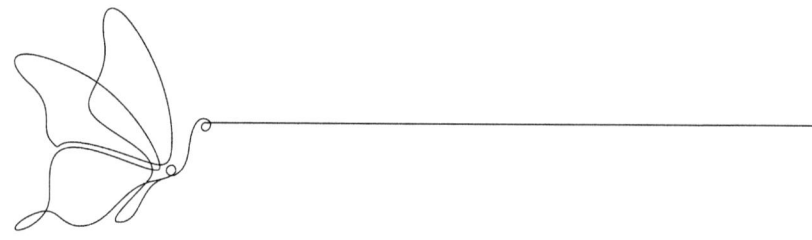

I am in my body
and feel the
sensations that come
up to guide me.

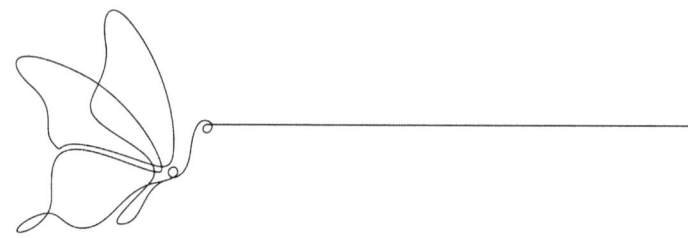

I am connected
to myself and those
around me.

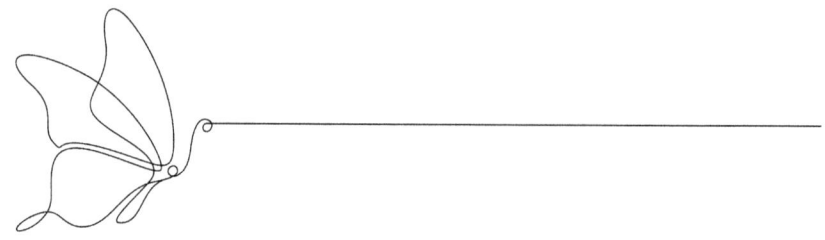

I am aware
of what sustains me
and avoid
what harms me.

I am purposeful
and seek satisfaction
in what I do.

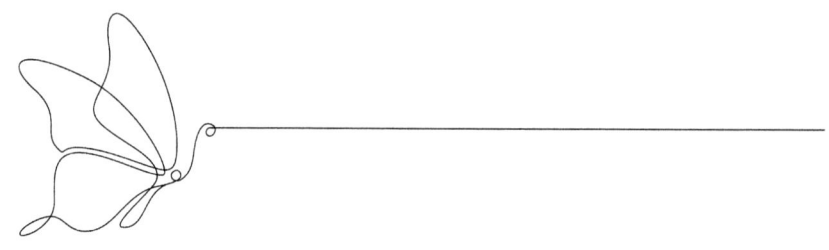

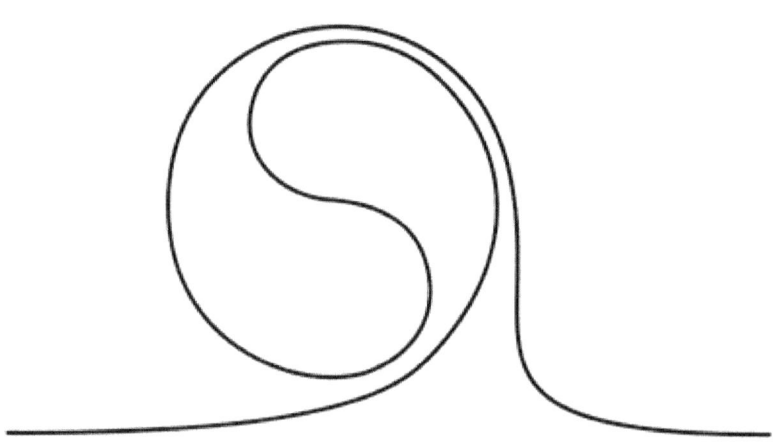

I am love
and I share
my gifts with
the world.

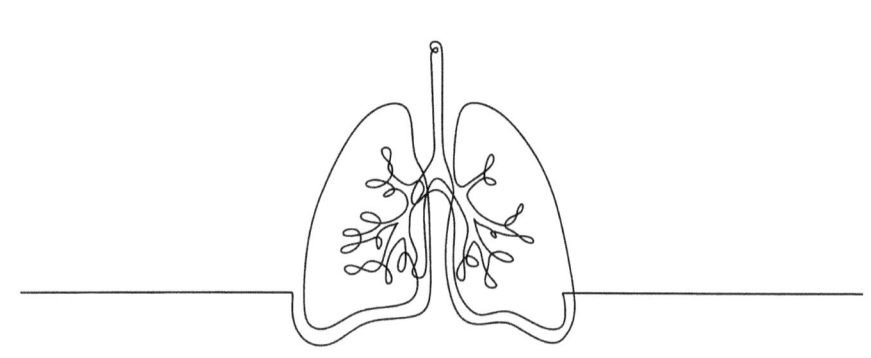

I am aware of
my body's brilliance
and tune into it
for messages.

Whatever **I am**
not changing,
I am choosing.

www.ingramcontent.com/pod-product-compliance
Lightning Source LLC
Chambersburg PA
CBHW060536130626
46553CB00002B/784